candlelight

Arranged by Brent Edstrom

contents

ISBN 978-1-4950-5476-1

7777 W. BLUEMOUND RD. P.O. BOX 13819 MILWAUKEE, WI 53213

AT LAST

Lyric by MACK GORDON
Music by HARRY WARREN

Slow Swing
C A7♯5 Dm7 G9 Em7 A7♯5
Dm7 G7 C6/E A7♯5 Dm7 Fm6
C6/9/E A7♯5 D7 G9sus G13 C A7♯5
Dm7 G9 Em7 A7♯5 Dm7 G7♯5
C6 A7♯5 Dm7 Fm6 C6 Fm7 G9sus(♯5) G9
C6/9 G♭9♯5 Fmaj9 G13sus G7♭9 Cmaj7
mf

F♯m11♭5
Em/B
B7
Em6
Am7♭5
D13sus
D7♭9
Gmaj7♯5
G6
Am7
D13♭9
G13sus
f
C
A7♯5
Dm7
G7♯5
G9sus
Em7
A7♯5
Dm7
G7♯5
C6/E
A7♯5
Dm7
G13
1.
C6
A7♯5
Dm7
D7
G7
G7♯5
2.
B♭13
A7♯5
ff
Dm7
C/G
C
C/E
F
F♯dim7
C/G
D♭9
C9
mf

THE BOY NEXT DOOR

Words and Music by HUGH MARTIN
and RALPH BLANE

A♭dim(maj7)
Gm7
Gm9
C13
Fmaj9
A♭dim(maj7)
Gm7
C9♯11
Cm7
mf
F13
F7♭9
B♭maj9
E♭13
mp
Fmaj7/C
D♭maj7♯11/C
cresc.
C9sus
Fmaj7/C
Moderate Swing Waltz
C9sus
mf
C6/9
F9sus
rit.
F13♭9
mp
B♭(add2)
f
D♭maj9
G♭maj13
C♭maj9
B♭maj9
D♭maj13
G♭maj13
F7♯9
mf
B♭maj7
G13♯11
Cm(add2)

F9♯11
B♭maj9
Gm9
Gm11/C
C13
Cm7
cresc.
F13
F9♯5
B♭maj7
Gm9
Em7♭5
A7♯5(♭9)
ff
Dm7
D♭13♯11
Cm7
F13
B♭maj9
mf
G13♯11
G7♯5(♭9)
Cm9
F9♯11
B♭maj9
Gm9
C13
To Coda
C9♯11
B♭maj7/F
A/G
Gm7
Cm9
Bm7
Cm7
B♭m9/E♭
Bm9/E
1.
Cm9/F
f
F13
mf
2.
Cm9/F
f

F7♯5(♯9) F7♯5(♭9) B♭maj7 G13 Cm7 F13
mf
B♭maj7 Gm7 C13sus C9sus C9 Cm7
F7 B♭6 Gm7 Em7♭5 A7♯5(♭9)
Dm9 D♭7♯5 Cm7 F13 B♭maj7 G13 Cm7
F13 B♭maj7 Gm9 C13 C13♯11
B♭maj7 G13 Cm9 F13 B♭m7
f

Gb13 F13 Bb6/9 Db13#11 C13#11 B13#11 Bb(add2)/F A/F Eb7sus/F E7sus/F
mp
Bb7sus/F G/F C#7sus/F D7sus/F D7sus/E B7sus/D Dbmaj13 Gm7/C Am7/C
cresc.
Bbm9/C Cm9 F9sus F13 F9#5 Bbmaj7 Gm11
mf
Em7b5 A7#5(b9) Eb13 Dm9 Db13#11 Cm7 F13b5
D.S. al Coda
CODA
Bm7 Cm7 Gb13 F7#11 Bb(add2) Dbmaj9
Straight 8ths
Gbmaj7 F13b9 Bb Cm7 F7sus Bb6
rit.
molto rit.
mp

CALL ME IRRESPONSIBLE

from the Paramount Picture PAPA'S DELICATE CONDITION

Words by SAMMY CAHN
Music by JAMES VAN HEUSEN

F6
F♯dim7
Gm6/9
G♯dim7
mf
Am
F/A
B♭7♯11
A7
D13sus
E♭9sus
D9sus
D7♯5(♯9)
f
F♯dim7
Gm7
Cdim7
C13
Am11
D13sus
D7♭5(♭9)
Gm11
Cdim7
C13
A9sus
E♭9
D9sus
D7♭9
Gm11
D♭13
3
C9sus
C7
mf
F(add2)/G
A♭m7
Gm7
G♭13
F
F♯dim7

Gm7
G♯dim7
Am9
D13sus
D7♭5(♭9)
f
G6
mf
G♯dim7
Am7
Am6
B♭dim7
G(add2)
B9
F9
E7♯5(♭9)
Am7
E♭7♯5
D7sus
D7
Bm7♭5
B♭7
Am7
B♭dim(maj7)/A
A13sus
A13
D7sus
Fdim7/D
Am7/D
D7♯5
G6
G♯dim7

Am6/9
A♯dim7
Bm
G/B
B9sus
B7
E13sus
E13
E♭13
E13
Am11
Am7
f
Ddim7
D13
Bm7♭5
E13sus
E7♭5(♭9)
Am11
Ddim7
D13
B9sus
F9
E9sus
E7♭9
Am11
D9sus
D9
mf
G
B♭6
A7
A♭maj7
G
B♭6
A7
A♭maj7
C
G
B♭m6
Am7
G(add2)
G6/9

DANCE ONLY WITH ME

Music by JULE STYNE
Lyrics by BETTY COMDEN
and ADOLPH GREEN

C9 C9♯5 C9 Fmaj13 A7♯5 Dm(add2) Dm(maj7) Gm11 C9
E♭9♯11 D9 D7♭9 G7♯5(♭9) C7♯5(♯9) C13♭9 Am(add2)
Lilting Swing
D9sus D7♯5(♯9) G13 C13 C9♯5 C7♯5(♭9) F6 Am7 D7♭5(♭9)
Gm7 C9 Am7 A♭13♯11 Gm7
C9 C7♭9 Em11 E♭13♯11 Dm(add2) Bm9 B♭7♯5(♯9)
Amaj9 F♯m9 D♯m7♭5 G♯7♭9 C♯m7

C13
Gm6/9
C13
C7♯5
Am11
D7♯9
Straight 8ths, with rubato
Gm11
C9
Am7♭5
D7♯5(♭9♯9)
G7♯5(♭9)
cresc.
f
mf
C7♯5(♯9)
Am7♭5
D7♭5(♭9)
G13
Swing, a tempo
C13(♯9)
C13♭9
F6/9
A♭13
mp
rall.
mf
D♭maj13
G♭13
F6/9
A♭13
D♭maj13
G♭13
Fmaj13
F6/9

HE WAS TOO GOOD TO ME

Words by LORENZ HART
Music by RICHARD RODGERS

Bright Swing
E♭6
Fm7
B♭9
Fm9
B♭9
mf
E♭6
Fm7
E♭6/G
E♭6
Fm7
B♭9
Fm9
B♭9
3
E♭6
E♭maj7/D
D♭13♯11
C9
A♭m6
F9
B♭9
E♭6/G
G♭dim7
Fm7
B♭13
E♭6
G♭13
B9
B♭13
E♭6
Fm7
B♭9
B9♯5
B♭9

Eb6
Fm7
Eb6/G
Eb6
Fm7
Bb9
Fm9
Bb9
Eb
Fm9
Eb/G
Eb7/Bb
Abm6
F7/A
Abm6
3
Eb6/Bb
Cm7
Fm7
Bb13
1.
Eb6
Am11b5
Fm11
Bb13
2.
Eb6
Gb13
B9
Bb13
Eb6/G
Gb13
B9#11
Bb13
Eb6
Abm6
Eb6

I HADN'T ANYONE TILL YOU

Words and Music by
RAY NOBLE

Gm9
C13♭5(♭9)
F(add2)
f
mf
Am7
G♯dim7
Am7
D13
G9
G13
G7♯5
B♭maj7
A7♯5(♯9)
E♭9♯11
Dm6/9
f
Bm7♭5
B♭7♯11
A6/9
B13
E13
A13
Adim7
3
Gm7
C9
Gm7
G♭9♯5
Gm7
C13
F6/9
B♭maj7/F
mf
Am7 Gm7
Fmaj7
Am7
A♭dim7
Am7
D13
G13
D♭9♯5

C9 B9 B♭6/9 D♭9 C13sus C13
f
Am7♭5 D7♭5(♭9) Gm7 F♯dim7 Gm7 C13 F(add2)
mf
f
E♭9 D9 B♭6/9 D♭9 F6 Gm7
Straight 8ths
Am7♭5 D7♭5(♭9)
8va
Freely
Gm9
rall.
mf
Flowing
C13 C13♭9 F6 F7♯9 B♭13 E♭7♯9 A♭13
mp
rit.
G13 G13(♭9) G♭13 F6/9

IF I HAD YOU

Words and Music by TED SHAPIRO,
JIMMY CAMPBELL and REG CONNELLY

Slightly faster
B♭6 Fm7 B♭9 E♭6 E♭m6 A♭13
mf
B♭ Dm D♭dim Cm7 F7♯5 B♭6/D D♭dim7
Cm7 F13 F7♯5 B♭6 Fm7 B♭9 E♭6
E♭m6 A♭9 B♭6 Dm D♭dim Cm7 F9♯5 B♭ B♭/D D♭dim7 Cm7
B♭6 A7 Dm6 Em7♭5 A7♭9 Dm(add2) Dm6/F
mp
B♭9♯11 A7♭9 Dm6 Dm(add2) Em7♭5 A7♯5 E♭9 Dm(add2) G13

Cm7
F9♯5
B♭6
Fm7
B♭9
E♭6
E♭m6
A♭9
B♭6
Dm
D♭dim
Cm7
F9♯5
To Coda
B♭
B♭/D
D♭dim
Cm7
B♭6
A7
Swing 16ths
Dm6
Em7♭5
A7♯5
Dm6
Em7♭5
A7♯5
Dm6
Swing 8ths
Em7♭5
A7♯5
Dm
Cm7
F7
D.S. al Coda
CODA
D9
G13
Cm7
F7
B♭
B♭/D
D♭dim7
Cm7
B♭
C♭6/9
B♭6/9
8vb

LAZY AFTERNOON

from the GOLDEN APPLE

Words and Music by JOHN LaTOUCHE
and JEROME MOROSS

Slowly, with rubato

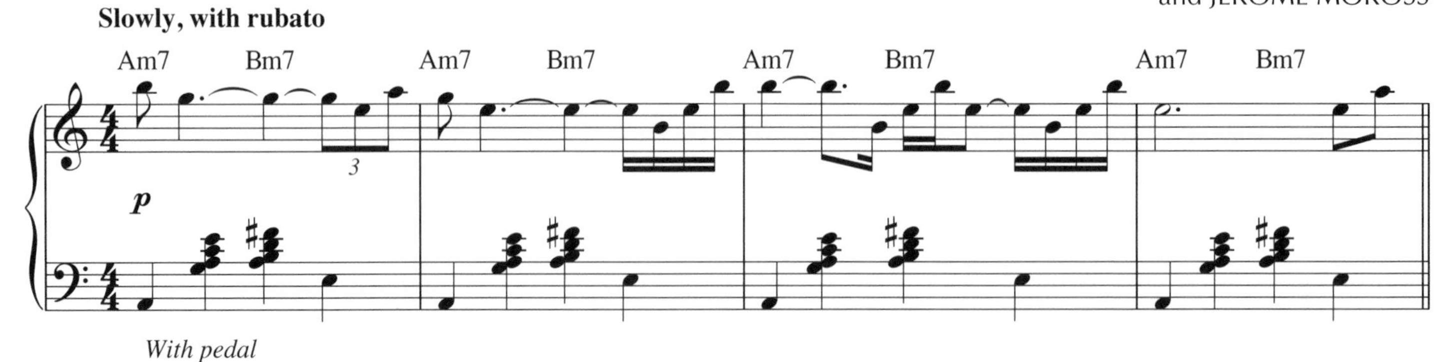

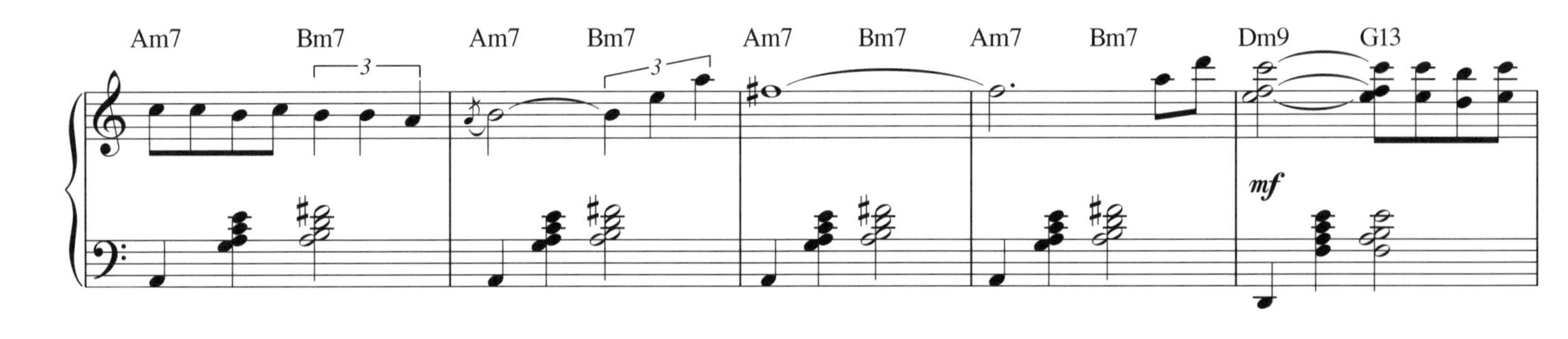

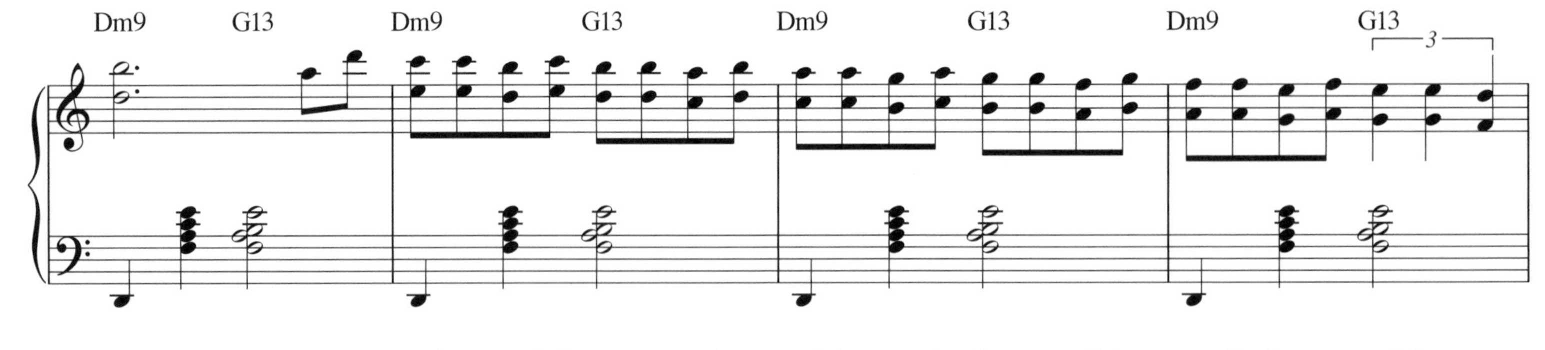

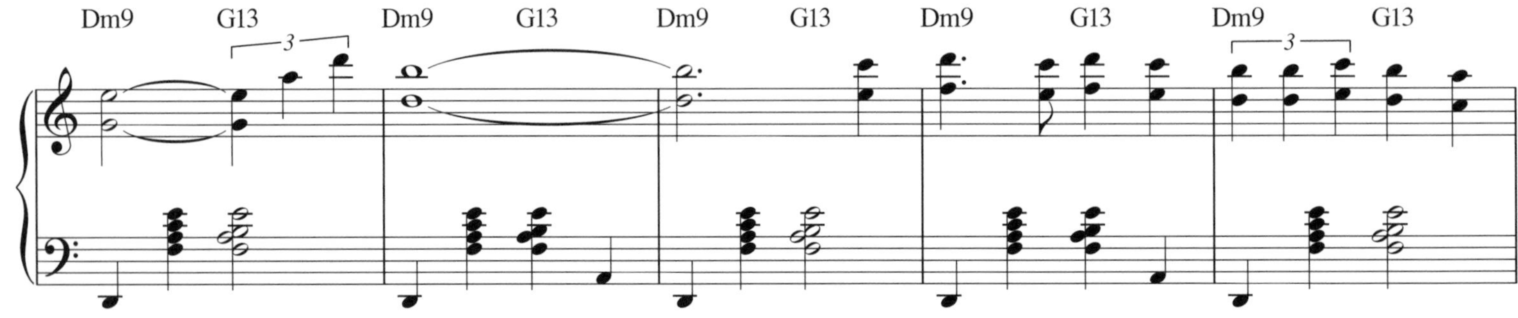

C6/9
F13♯11
Em7
E♭7♯11
Dm9
G13
Cmaj7
3
Bm7♭5
E7♯5(♯9)
mp
Am7
Bm7
Am7
Bm7
Am7
Bm7
3
Am7
Bm7
Am7
Bm7
Am7
Bm7
Am7
Bm7
rit.
Am7
Bm7
p
Medium Swing
Am7
D9
mf
Am7
D9
Am7
D9
Am7
D9
Am7
D9
Am7
D9
Am7
D9
Am7
D9
Am7
D9
Am7
D9
Am7
D9
Am7
D9

Dm9
G13
Dm9
G13
Dm9
G13
Dm9
G13
Dm9
G13
Dm9
G13
Dm9
G13
Dm9
G13
Dm9
f
G13sus
G13
Cmaj7
F7♯11
Em7
A7
Dm13
G13sus
G13
C
Bm7♭5
E7♯5(♯9)
Am7
D9
mf
Am7
D9
Am7
D9
Am7
D9
Am7
D9
Am7
D9
Am7
D9
Am7
D9
Am7
D9
Am7
D9

To Coda
Am7 D9 Am7 D9 Am7 D9 Am7 D9
Am7 D9 Am7 D9 Am7 D9 Am7 D9
Am7 D9 Am7 D9 Am7 D9 Am7 E♭13♯11
Dm9 G13 Dm9 G13 Dm9 G13 Dm9 G13
f
Dm9 G13 Dm9 G13 Dm9 G13 Dm9 G13
Dm9 G13 Cmaj7 F7♯11 Em7 E♭13♯11

Dm9
G13sus
G13
C6/9
Bm7♭5
E7♯5(♯9)
Am7
D9
Am7
D9
Am7
D9
mf
Am7
D9
Am7
D9
Am7
D9
Am7
D9
D.S.al Coda
Am7
D9
Am7
D9
Am7
D9
Am7
D9
CODA
Am9
D9
Am9
D9
Am9
D9
Am9
D9
decresc.
Am7
D9
Am7
D9
Am6/9
mp
p

LET THERE BE YOU

Words and Music by VICKI YOUNG
and DAVID CAVANAUGH

Relaxed Swing
D9
G7
G7♭9
Cmaj9
Gm7
C7
Fmaj7
F♯dim7
Cmaj9/G
Cmaj9
A13
B♭13
A13
Dm7
G9sus
C(add2)
Am9
D9
G9sus
G13♭9
C(add2)/E
E♭dim7
Dm7
f
To Coda
G13
G7♯5
Cmaj9
Bm11
B♭13
A13
A7♯5
Dm7
Dm6
D9
G7
G7♭9
C6/9
B♭13
C6/9
B♭13
C6
B♭6
mf
A♭13
G13
C6
E♭9
D9♯11
G13
G7♯5

Cmaj9
Bm7
B♭9♯11
A13
E♭9♯11
Dm7
Dm6
Am9
D9
Dm9
G13♭9
Cmaj9
E♭dim7
Dm7
G9
mp
B♭13♯11
A13
B♭13
A13
Dm5
D9
G7
G7♭9
mf
D.S. al Coda
CODA
Cmaj9
Gm7
C7
A13
A7♯5
Dm7
Dm6
cresc.
D9
G7
G7♭9
B♭9♯11
A7♯5(♭9)
D9
f
G13sus
C7
C6
D♭maj13
C6
mf

THE MAN WITH THE HORN

Lyric by EDDIE DE LANGE
Music by JACK JENNEY, BONNIE LAKE
and EDDIE DE LANGE

A♭maj7 A♭m7 D♭7♭9 D♭7♯5(♭9) G♭maj7 A♭m7
f
B♭m7 A♭m7 G♭maj7 Cm11 F13 Cm9 F13 B♭13sus B9♯5
B♭13sus G13♯9 C7♯9 C7♭9 Fm9 B♭9 Cm7
mf
F13 Cm9 F13 F9♯11 B♭13sus A♭maj7 Gm7 F♯m7
B♭13sus Fm9 E7♯9
1.
E♭(add2) F♯m9 B13 B♭13sus
f mf
2.
E♭(add2) Fm9 B♭13 E♭(add2) E♭6 Fm7 E♭6/G Fm7

E♭6
Fm
F♯m
E♭6/G
G♭dim7
Fm7
B♭13
B7
B♭9
E♭6/G
G♭dim7
B♭7
E♭6
Fm7
Double time feel, Swing 16ths
E♭6/G
Fm7
E♭6
Fm7
E♭/G
C9
Fm7
B♭9
Swing 8ths
Fm7
B♭9
E♭6
A♭9♯11
E♭6
E♭13♭9
A♭maj7
f
A♭m7
D♭9
G♭maj13
B9
Cm7
F13
D♭m7
Cm9
F13
B♭13sus
B♭13
mf
E♭6
Fm7

Eb6/G
C9
F9
G7#5
F9
Fm7
Bb13
Fm7
Bb13
Eb9
D9
Eb9
D9
Eb9
D9 Eb13
cresc.
f
Abmaj7
Abm7
Db7b9
Db7#5(b9)
Gbmaj7
Abm9
Bbm7
Abm7
Gbmaj7
Cm7
F9
Cm9
F9
Bb9sus
B9#5
Bb13sus
mf
Ebmaj9
Abmaj7/Eb
Ebmaj7
Cm7
F13
Cm9
F9#11
Bb9sus
Abmaj7
Gm7
F#m7
Fm9
E7#9
Eb6
Ab13#11
Ebmaj7

MAYBE YOU'LL BE THERE

Words by SAMMY GALLOP
Music by RUBE BLOOM

E♭maj9 Cm9 Edim7 Fm11 B♭7♯5 E♭6 Cm7 Dm7 G7
A♭maj9 D♭9♯11 E♭6 C7♯5 F9 B♭13sus B♭13 E♭6/9
f
B♭7 E♭6 C7♯5 Fm
Gm11♭5 C7♭9 Fm F9 B9 B♭9♯5
To Coda
E♭maj7 E♭maj7/G Edim7 Fm11 B♭9♯5 E♭6 Cm7 Dm11 G9
A♭maj9 D♭9♯11 E♭maj9/G C9 Fm7 B♭13 E♭6 B♭13♭9

Emaj13
C7
Fm7
B♭9
E♭7
Dm7♭5
G7
mf
A♭maj7
D♭9♯11
E♭maj7
E♭7
C7♯5
F9
B9♯11
B♭9
E♭maj13
C9
Fm11
B♭13
E♭6
Dm11
G7♯5
f
A♭maj7
D♭9♯11
E♭maj13
C7♯5
F9
B9♯5
B♭13
E♭6
D.S. al Coda
CODA
A♭maj9
D♭9♯11
E♭maj9/G
C9
Fm7
B9♯5
B♭13
E♭6
mf

OVER THE RAINBOW

from THE WIZARD OF OZ

Music by HAROLD ARLEN
Lyric by E.Y. "YIP" HARBURG

A♭m/B♭
E♭maj9
Fm7
B9♯11
B♭7sus
B♭13
Slow and steady
E♭
Cm
Gm
E♭13
A♭maj9
A♭13
A♭7♯5
Gm7
C7♭9
mf
Fm9
A♭m6
Gm7
C9
C7♯5(♭9)
B7♭5(♯9)
B♭9
B♭13♭9
A♭
G♭6
F7
Emaj7
E♭(add2)
E♭6
Gm7
E♭13
A♭maj9
Am7♭5
D7♭5(♭9)
Gm7
C7♭5
C7
A♭maj9
D♭9
E♭maj7/B♭
C9
C7♯5(♭9)
B♭9
B♭7♭9
E♭(add2)
E♭maj7
Fm11
B♭9
E♭6
mp

E♭maj7
F9
Gm7
E♭dim(maj7)
Fm7
B♭9
B♭7♯5
cresc.
Am7♭5
D7♭5(♭9)
Gm
B♭13
A♭maj9
Am7♭5
D7♭5(♭9)
f
Gm9
C7♭5(♯9)
A♭maj9
A♭m6
E♭/B♭
C7♯9
C7♯5(♭9)
Fm7
B♭9sus
B♭13♭9
1.
E♭(add2)
B♭13sus
2.
E♭6/9
mp
E♭
Fm7/E♭
E♭6
A♭(add2)
E♭maj9/B♭
E♭6/B♭
B♭7
rit.
E♭6

NEVER NEVER LAND

from PETER PAN

Lyric by BETTY COMDEN and ADOLPH GREEN
Music by JULE STYNE

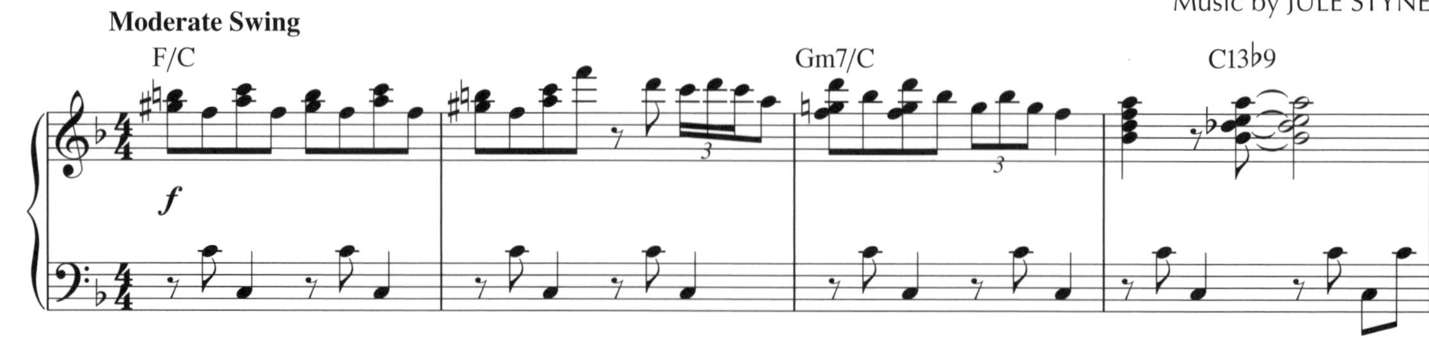

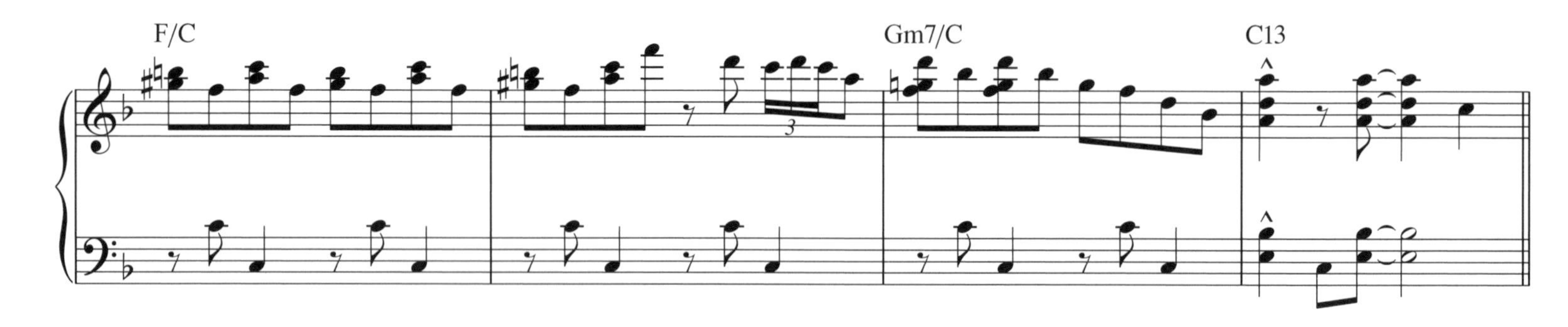

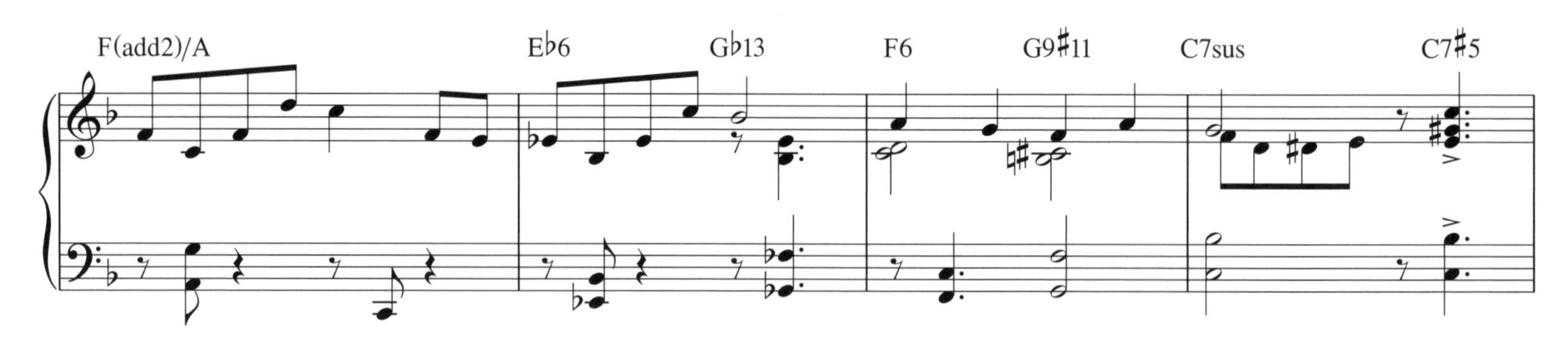

F(add2)/A Eb6 Gb13 F6 Gm7 C7b9 Bb/F F Eb7
Abmaj7 Bbm7 Eb9 Eb7b9 Abmaj7 Gb6 C9
f
To Coda
Fmaj7 Fdim(maj7) C9sus Cdim7 G9 C9
F F6 Bbmaj7 Bbm(maj7) Am7 Dm7 Gdim7/D Bm7b5 Bbm6
mf
F(add2)/A Eb6 Eb9
1.
Dm7 F7 Bb6 C9sus
F/C Db9 C9
2.
Dm F7 Gm7 Edim7 Gm7 Edim7

F/C
Gb13
F
f
mf
Am7
Dm7
Bm7b5
Bbm6
F
Gb6
G9
Gm7
C7
F
Bb6
Am7
Dm7
Bm7b5
Bbm7
Eb7/Bb
F(add2)
Gbmaj9#11
Eb13
Gb13
C13sus
Bbm/C
Bb/F
F
Abmaj7
Bbm7
Eb9
Abmaj7
Gbmaj7
Gb13
F
Fdim(maj7)

Gm7 C7 D♭7 C7♭5 F Gm7 C13 G♭
f
F Dm7 Bm7♭5 E♭9 F(add2)/A F G♭
D.S. al Coda
G9sus G♭7 F A A♭ G G♭(add2)
CODA
F F/E♭ E♭9♯11
mf
Am7 Dm7 Bm7♭5 B♭m6 F(add2)/A E♭6 E♭9
Dm7 F7 B♭ Adim7 Gm7 G♭9♯11 F F/E♭
f
D♭maj7 F F7♯11
mf

ONCE UPON A TIME

from the Broadway Musical ALL AMERICAN

Lyric by LEE ADAMS
Music by CHARLES STROUSE

B♭maj7
D7♯5(♯9)
Gm
Gm(add2)
Gm(maj7)/D
E♭maj9
B♭6
E♭maj7
Am7
D7
Gm7
f
E♭maj7
F9sus
F13♭9
B♭6
Cm7/F
B♭maj9
B♭6
Cm7
F7
B♭maj7
mf
Cm7
F7
B♭maj7
Am7
D7
Gm7
C7sus
C7
F7sus
F13
F9/E♭
B♭6/D
F9/E♭
Gm7/D
Gm9
C13
F9sus
F13
F7♯5
B♭maj7
Gm7
Gm(maj7)
Gm7

To Coda
E♭maj9
B♭6
E♭maj7
E♭6
Am7
D7
Gm
E♭maj9
Cm9
F7sus
F13♭9
B♭6
F13sus
F13
B♭maj9
D9sus
D7♭5(♭9)
Gm9
Gm9/F
mf
E♭6/9
B♭maj9
E♭6/9
Am7♭5
D7♯5(♯9)
Gm
Gm(♯5)
B♭maj9/F
F13sus
F13
B♭maj7
Gm9
Gm7/F

E♭6/9
B♭maj7
E♭6/9
B♭maj9
Gm
F13sus
F13
B♭maj7
A♭13♯11
D.S. al Coda
CODA
Gm
E♭maj9
Cm9
F9
F13♭9
f
D7♯9
A♭13
G7♯5
Cm7
F13♭9
A♭9
G7♯5(♯9)
ff
Cm9
F9sus
F13♭9
B♭(add2)
A♭6♯11
G♭6♯11
A♭6/9
B♭(add2)
dim.
mf

SEND IN THE CLOWNS

from the Musical A LITTLE NIGHT MUSIC

Words and Music by
STEPHEN SONDHEIM

Ebmaj7/Bb
Bb9sus
Eb6/9
Fm11
Ebmaj7
Bb9sus
Swing 8ths
Eb(add2)
mf
Abmaj7/Eb
Eb(add2)
Abmaj7/Eb
3
Ebmaj9
Eb9sus
Eb9
Abmaj7
Ebmaj7/Bb
Bb9sus
Ebmaj7/Bb
Bb9sus
Eb(add2)
Abmaj7/Eb
Eb(add2)
Dm11

Gm11
f
E♭maj9
Dm11
Gm11
Dm11
Gm11
F6/9
E♭maj9♯11
Cm7
G/B
E♭(add2)/B♭
F(add2)/A
A♭maj7
G9sus
3
Fm7♭5
Gm9
mf
B♭9sus
E♭maj9/B♭
Straight 8ths
B♭9sus
E♭(add2)
mp

B♭9sus
E♭(add2)
B♭9sus
E♭maj9
E♭9
A♭maj7
D♭maj9
G♭6/9
E♭maj7/B♭
B♭9sus
E♭maj7/B♭
B♭9sus
1.
E♭maj13
Fm11/E♭
E♭maj13
A♭maj7/E♭
Swing 8ths
E♭(add2)
A♭maj7/E♭
E♭(add2)
Dm11
2.
E♭sus(add2)
p
B♭13sus
E♭
E♭sus
E♭
8vb

THE SHADOW OF YOUR SMILE

Love Theme from THE SANDPIPER

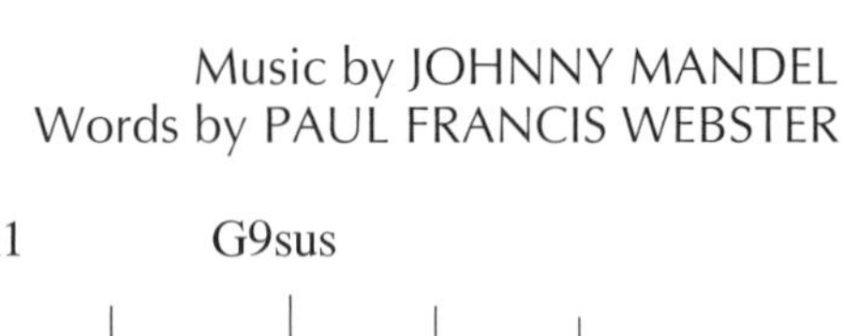

Relaxed Bossa groove
Am/G
G
F♯m9
B7sus
B7♭9
mp
mf
Em9
A9
Am
D9
Gmaj7♯5
G6
Cmaj9
F♯m7♭5
B7sus
B7♭9
Em
Em(maj7)
Em7
C♯m7♭5
F♯9
F♯7♭9
B9sus
B9
F♯m7
B9
B7♭9
Em9
A9
Am7
D9
D7♭9

Bm7♭5
E7♭5(♯9)
E9♯5
Am7
Cm7
F13♯11
f
Bm7
F13♯11
E9
E7♯5(♭9)
A9
E♭9♯11
Am7
D13sus
D7♭9
G6/9
F♯m11♭5
B7♯5(♯9)
mf
Adim7/E
Em7
A13
Am7
D9
Gmaj7
Cmaj7
F♯m7♭5
B7
Em
C♯m7♭5
F♯7♭9

B13 C13 B13 B♭13
B13
f
mf
F♯m9
B13
Em
A13
Am7
D9
Bm7♭5
E7♭9
Am7
Cm7
F13
Bm7
F9♯11
E9
E7♯5(♭9)
A9
E♭9♯11
Am7
D13
D7♭9
G(add2)
F6/9
decresc.
E♭maj7
F6/9
G(add2)
F6/9
rit.
Emaj7
mp

SPRING CAN REALLY HANG YOU UP THE MOST

Lyric by FRAN LANDENSMAN
Music by TOMMY WOLF

Steady Ballad tempo
D9
G9
G7♭9
C6/9
B♭(add2)
C6/9
B♭maj9
Am9
Dm7
G9
mp
Em7
A7♭5(♭9)
F♯m7♭5
Fm6
C/E
A♭9♯11
mf
Dm7
D♭(♯11)
C
D♭/C
Cmaj9
B♭6/9
C(add2)
B♭6/9
mp
Cmaj7/G
G9sus
G7
Em7
A7♭5(♭9)
F♯m7♭5
Fm6
C/E
A♭9♯11
Dm9
G7
G7♭9
Cmaj7
Gm7
Cmaj9/G
Gm7
Cmaj7/G
Gm7
C6/9/G
mf

Gm7
C6/9/G
Cm7
C6
Cm7
C6
F♯m11♭5
B7/F♯
Emaj7
Am9
D7
Gmaj7
Fmaj9
C
B♭6
Am9
G9sus
Em7
E♭7
F♯m7♭5
Fm6
C/E
A♭9♯11
Dm9
G9
8va
B♭13
A7♭5(♭9)
G13sus
D♭(♯11)
C
B♭13
Double time, Swing 8ths
C6/9
B♭13
C6/9
B♭13

Am9
Dm7
G7
Em7
A7♯5(♯9)
F♯m7♭5
Fm9
Am9
D7sus
D13
Dm9
G7♯5(♭9)
C6/9
B♭9
C6/9
B♭13
C6/9
B♭13
Em7
Dm7
G9
Em7
A13
F♯m7♭5
Fm6
C6/9/E
D9

G7sus G9sus Dm11 G13 C6/9 B♭9
3
C9sus C6/9 C9sus C6/9
mp
C9sus Cmaj13 C9sus
cresc.
3
Cmaj9 Cm7 D♭maj13 Cm11
mf
D♭maj7♯11 F♯m11♭5 B7/F♯ Emaj7 Emaj13
mp
cresc.
Half time, straight 8ths
Am9 D9 D7♭9 G(add2) F6/9 Cmaj9 B♭6/9
mf

Am9
Dm7
G9
Em7
A7♭9
F♯m7♭5
Fm7
E♭m11
A♭9sus
A♭7♭9
Dm9
G9
B♭13♯11
A7♭9
G9sus
Cmaj9/G
mp
G7sus
Cmaj9/G
Bm7♭5
B♭9
Am9
D13sus
D13♯11
mf
mp
Dm9
B♭13
Em
A9
Dm11
D♭
C6/9
D♭/C
C6/9
rit. e dim.
p

THAT'S ALL

Words and Music by BOB HAYMES
and ALAN E. BRANDT

B♭maj9/F
Cm11/F
F13♭9
B♭maj9/F
Fdim7
Cm11/F
F13♭9
B♭maj9
E♭maj13
Dm7
G9
G13
Em7♭5
E♭9
D7♯5(♯9)
G13♯9
G7♯5(♯9)
Cm11
F13♭5(♭9)
E♭(add2)
G♭13
B♭6
E7♯11
f
B♭13sus
B♭13
E♭maj7
Fm7
Gm7
G♭9
B♭13sus
B♭13
E♭maj7
Fm7
Gm7
Fm7
E♭maj7
E♭6

C13sus
C13
Fmaj7
B♭maj9
Am7♭5
D7♭9
ff
C13sus
C13
Cm11
F13
B7♯9
fff
mf
B♭maj9
Cm11
F13
Dm7
G9
Cm11
F13
B♭maj9
Cm11
F13
Dm7
G9
G13
Em7♭5
E♭9
D7♯5(♯9)
G13♯9
G7♯5(♯9)
Dm7
D♭7
Cm11
F13♭9
1.
E♭
Dm7 Cm7 Dm7
B♭

2.
E♭
Dm Cm Dm
B♭
mp
Em7♭5
E♭maj7
D7♯5
D♭13
f
Cm7
F7
B♭6
Fm11
B♭13
ff
Em7♭5
mp
E♭maj9
D7♯5
G13♯9
F9sus
mf
F13sus
F13
B♭6
C♭6/9
B♭6/9
mp

TOO LATE NOW

Words by ALAN JAY LERNER
Music by BURTON LANE

𝄋
Bm7 E7♯5(♯9) Am(maj7) Am6 Bm7 E9 Am(maj7)
f
To Coda
Am11 D7♯5(♯9) Gm(maj7) Gm6 Am6 D9 G9sus G7♭5(♭9)
3
Cmaj7 G9sus G7sus(♭9) Cmaj7 Dm11 G9sus
mp
Cmaj7 Am9 F♯m7♭5 F9♯11 Em7 A7♭9 G9sus G7♭9
f
mf
Cmaj7 Cdim(maj7) E♭m7 A♭13 A♭7♯5
Gentle rhythm
D♭maj7 B♭m9 E♭m11 A♭13♭9
mp
Fm7 Em9 A7 E♭m9 A♭13♭9 D♭6 B♭m7 Gm7♭5 C7♭9
3

Fmaj7
B♭9♯11
E♭m7
A♭13♭9
D♭maj9
B♭m9
E♭m9
A♭9sus
D♭maj9
B♭m9
E♭m11
F7♯9
F7♭9
B♭m9
B♭m9/A♭
Gm7♭5
C7♯5(♯9)
D.S. al Coda
Fm7
B♭7♭9
Em11
A9
Dm11
G9
C(add2)
CODA
Cmaj9
Am9
Dm9
G9sus
B♭9♯11
Am9
G9sus
E7♯9
E7♭9
Am
Am9/G
F♯m7♭5
B7♯5
Em7
A7♭9
G9sus
G7♭9
F♯m7♭5
Fm6
mf
Cmaj7/E
E♭m7
D7♯11
D♭9♯11
D♭7♯9(♯11)
C(add2)
rit.

UNCHAINED MELODY

Lyric by HY ZARET
Music by ALEX NORTH

C
G
G7
Am
Am7/G
Em
A9
F6
G9
C
C7
F/C
C6
F
G
F
E♭maj7
F
G
C9
D♭9
C9
f
F
G
F
E♭maj7
F
G
C7
Gm7
C
C/D
E7
Am7
Am/G
F6/9
G13
C6
E7
Am7
Am/G
G13
A♭13
Fmaj9
ff

G13
C
E7♯5
Am7
Am/G
f
F6
G9
C6
E7
Am7
G13
A♭13
G13
A♭13
G13
C13
cresc.
ff
f
G7
E7
Am7
Am7/G
Em
F6
mf
G9
C6
E7
Am9
Am/G
Straight 8ths
Fmaj7
F6
Fm6
C
ff

THE WINDMILLS OF YOUR MIND

Theme from THE THOMAS CROWN AFFAIR

Words by ALAN and MARILYN BERGMAN
Music by MICHEL LEGRAND

A♯dim7
B7sus
B7
Em
Am
D7
Gmaj7
cresc.
Dm
G9
Cmaj7
f
F♯7
Bm
Bm/A
E/G♯
E7
Am7
Am/G
D7
Gmaj7
Cmaj7
F♯m7♭5
dim.
B7sus
B7
Em
mf
F♯m7♭5
B7sus
B7♯5
A♯dim7
Em/B
To Coda

B7sus
B7
Em
F#m7b5
B7
Em
D
C
B
f
Em
F#m7b5
B7
Em6
B7#5
Em
F#m7b5
B7
Em
mf
C7
B7
Em
Em/D#
Dm
Em/C#
C13
D13
C13
B7#5
cresc.
f
D.S. al Coda
CODA
B7sus
B7
Em
F#m7b5
B7
cresc.
Em
D
C
B7
Em
f
ff

THE WAY YOU LOOK TONIGHT

Words by DOROTHY FIELDS
Music by JEROME KERN

2.
F7♯11 B♭9sus D♭9♯11 C9 A♭m9 D♭9 G♭maj7
f
Gdim7 A♭m9 D9♯11 D♭9 G♭6/9
B♭m9 Adim7 D♭13sus D♭9sus D♭9♯5(♯9) G♭maj7
Gdim7 A♭m11 D♭13 D♭7♭9 G♭6/9
E♭m9 B♭13sus B♭13 E♭maj9 E♭6
mf
Fm7 B13 B♭9sus B♭9 E♭maj7 D♭13

C7sus C7
Fm7 B♭9sus B♭13 Fm7/E♭
cresc.
f
E♭9 A9♯11
Fm7 B♭13sus B♭9 E♭6
dim.
mf
Fm9 B♭9 E♭6 Fm7 B♭9
A♭6 G7♯5 D♭13 C7♯5(♯9) B♭13sus B♭9 E♭6 G♭13
cresc.
f
F7♯11 B♭9sus D♭13♯11 C7♭5(♯9) C♭maj9 B♭13
mf
E♭ D♭(add2) Emaj7 D(♭9) E♭

YESTERDAY, WHEN I WAS YOUNG
(Hier Encore)

English Lyric by HERBERT KRETZMER
Original French Text and Music by
CHARLES AZNAVOUR

Gm9
C7
C7sus
C7
Fmaj7
B♭maj7
Gm
A7♯5
E♭13
Dm(add2)
D7
Gm
C7sus
C7
Fmaj7
B♭maj7
Gm
A7♭9
Steady Bossa groove
Dm(add2)
Dm(add2)♯5
Dm(add2)
dim.
Gm(add2)
mp
C7
B♭/F
Fmaj7
B♭maj7
Em11♭5
A7♯5
E♭9♯11
Dm
Dm♯5
Dm
D7♭5(♭9)
mf

Gm(add2)
C9
Fmaj7
B♭maj7
Em7♭5
A7sus
A7
Dm
Dm♯5
Dm(add2)
D7♭9
Gm9
C7sus
C7
Fmaj7
B♭maj7
Gm7
A7
Dm
Dm(♯5)
D7
Gm
C7
Fmaj7
B♭maj7
f
Gm(add2)
A7♯5
E♭13
Dm
Dm♯5
Dm(add2)
D.S. al Coda
mp

CODA
Dm
Dm♯5
Gm
A7sus
A7
Dm(add2)
Dm(add2)/C
decresc.
G/B
Gm6/B♭
Dm/A
Dm(add2)/A
rit.
a tempo
B♭6
D5
p
Em11♭5
cresc.
A7♯5(♭9)
mp
Em11♭5
A7♯5
Dm
Dm♯5
Dm
Dm(add2)
p
8vb

YOU ARE MY LUCKY STAR

Words by ARTHUR FREED
Music by NACIO HERB BROWN

Fmaj7
F(add2)
F
G9
C9sus
C13
F
B♭/D
Bdim7
C7
cresc.
Fmaj7
F(add2)
C
C7sus
C
mf
To Coda
Fmaj7
F(add2)
F6
Cm7
F7♭9
B♭maj9
E♭13

Fmaj7
C7
F
p
cresc.
F13
f
C7
F13
G7

C7
C7sus
C7♭5
C7
F
B♭
Bdim7
C7
F
C7
F
F7
B♭
E♭9
F
C
F
B♭/F
Fdim7
F
p
cresc.

D.S. al Coda
CODA
F13
Cm7
F9
F7♭9
B♭maj13
E♭13
cresc.
Fmaj7
C7
F
f
mp
Fdim7
Gm7/F
Fdim7
F6
B♭9/F
mf
Gm7/C
E♭maj9
E7♭9
F6
ff

YOU MUST BELIEVE IN SPRING

Lyrics by Alan and MARILYN BERGMAN
Music by MICHEL LEGRAND

Em7
A9sus
A7♭9
Gdim/D
D
G♯m7♭5
C♯7sus(♭9)
C♯7♭9
Gm7♭5
C7sus(♭9)
C7♭9
mf
Fm7
B♭7sus(♭9)
B♭9
E♭sus
Dm7♭5
G7♭9
Dm11♭5
G7sus(♭9)
G7♭9
mp
Gm7
A♭dim7
Am7♭5
E♭6/B♭
Fm7
B♭7sus(♭9)
B♭9
B♭7♭9
E♭maj13
Am7♭5
D7sus(♭9) D7♭9
mf
Gm7♭5
C7sus(♭9)
C7♭9
Fm7
B♭7sus(♭9)
B♭9
E♭sus
A♭maj9♯11
dim.
Dm11♭5
G7sus(♭9) G7♭9
Cm
mp
Dm7♭5
F♯m7♭5
B7♭9

C♯m7♭5
F♯7/B
Bm
Bm7
Em
A7sus
A7
A7♭9
Dmaj7
G♯m7♭5
C♯7sus
C♯7
F♯m7♭5
B7sus
B7♭9
Em7
A13sus
Dmaj7
C♯m7♭5
F♯7♯5(♯9)
C♯m7♭5
C13
F♯7/B
Bm
Em7
A9/E
A7♭9
Dmaj13
G♯m7♭5
C♯7sus
C♯7♭9
Gm7♭5
mf
C7
Fm9
B♭13
B♭7♯5
E♭6
Dm7♭5
D♭/G
Dm11♭5
mp
G7♭9
Cm/G
Cm
Cm/B♭

Fm9 B♭9 A♭m/E♭ E♭maj13 Am7♭5 D7♯5(♯9)
3
mf
3
Gm7♭5 C7♯5(♯9) Fm11♭5 B♭9 B♭7♭9 A♭/E♭ A♭maj9♯11
3
3
Dm11♭5 G7sus(♭9) G7 Cm Cm(add2) Cm(add2)/B♭ Am7♭5 A♭13♯11
dim.
mp
Gsus G F♯m7♭5 B7sus(♭9) B7 B7/E Em Am7 D7sus D7
p
mp
Cm/G Gmaj7 C♯m7♭5 F♯7sus(♭9) F♯7♭9 Bm7♭5 E9sus E9
mf
Am7 D9sus D7♭9 C/G F♯m7♭5 B7 F♯m7♭5 B7sus B7♭9 Adim/B Em Em/D
mp

Am7 D9sus D7♭9 F♯dim7/G G C♯m7♭5 F♯7sus(♭9) F♯7♭9
mf
Cm7♭5 F7sus(♭9) F7♭9 B♭m7 E♭9sus E♭9 D♭/A♭ Gm7♭5 C7♭9 Gm7♭5 C7sus(♭9) C7♭9
mp
Cm Cm/D♭ Dm7♭5 B♭m7 E♭9sus E♭9 D♭dim/E♭ A♭maj13
Dm7♭5 G7sus(♭9) G7♭9 Cm7♭5 F7sus(♭9) F7♭9 B♭m7 E♭9sus E♭9
mf
D♭/A D♭maj9♯11 Gm11♭5 C7sus(♭9) C7♭9 Fm D♭maj7
dim.
mp
3
D♭/C C Fm D♭/F B/F A/F Fm(add2)
p
dim.
pp
3
3